Looking at ...
Dilophosaurus

A Dinosaur from the JURASSIC Period

Weekly Reader®
BOOKS

Published by arrangement with Gareth Stevens, Inc.
Newfield Publications is a federally registered trademark
of Newfield Publications, Inc. Weekly Reader is a federally
registered trademark of Weekly Reader Corporation.

Library of Congress Cataloging-in-Publication Data

Brown, Mike, 1947-
    Looking at-- Dilophosaurus / written by Mike Brown; illustrated by Tony Gibbons.
        p. cm. -- (The New dinosaur collection)
    Includes index.
    ISBN 0-8368-1141-0
    1. Dilophosaurus--Juvenile literature. [1. Dilophosaurus. 2. Dinosaurs.] I. Gibbons, Tony,
ill. II. Title. III. Series.
QE862.S3B77 1994
567.9'7--dc20   94-16968

This North American edition first published in 1994 by
Gareth Stevens Publishing
1555 North RiverCenter Drive, Suite 201
Milwaukee, Wisconsin 53212 USA

This U.S. edition © 1994 by Gareth Stevens, Inc. Created with original © 1994 by
Quartz Editorial Services, Premier House, 112 Station Road, Edgware HA8 7AQ U.K.

Consultant: Dr. David Norman, Director of the Sedgwick Museum of Geology,
University of Cambridge, England.

Additional artwork by Clare Herronneau.

Printed in the United States of America

Looking at ...
Dilophosaurus
A Dinosaur from the JURASSIC Period

by Mike Brown

Illustrated by Tony Gibbons

THE NEW
DINOSAUR
COLLECTION

Gareth Stevens Publishing
MILWAUKEE

Contents

Introducing
Dilophosaurus

Let's travel far back in time – back to about 190 million years ago, to the Early Jurassic Period and to a place now known as Arizona.

If you were able to do this, you would probably meet **Dilophosaurus** (DIE-<u>LOAF</u>-OH-<u>SAW</u>-RUS), one of the earliest, giant, two-legged meat-eaters.

There are lots of interesting questions we might ask about this dinosaur.

What, for example, were the strange, platelike crests on **Dilophosaurus**'s head used for? Did **Dilophosaurus** spend any of its life in water? And could it defend itself by spitting poison at its enemies, as it does when recreated by scientists in the film *Jurassic Park*? Or is this a fantasy?

In the pages that follow, you will learn a great deal about this fascinating dinosaur. Join us, then, as we go on the trail of a fearsome, sharp-toothed carnivore.

Jurassic
monster

The first thing
you would have
noticed about
Dilophosaurus
was its size.

This large
dinosaur
measured
about 20
feet (6 m) in length.
Standing on two legs,
it would have towered
above you.

Such a huge monster would have been terrifying. But even in your fright, you would have been able to tell this was a **Dilophosaurus** right away.

Take a look at **Dilophosaurus**'s head. On the top of its head, you would have seen two thin crests of bone shaped like half-moons. They lay side by side and ran from the front to the back of the skull. These crests, or ridges, gave **Dilophosaurus** its name, which means "two-ridged lizard."

Look now at **Dilophosaurus**'s neck. It was very strong and flexible. **Dilophosaurus** needed a neck that moved easily for tearing meat and for peering around as it searched for food.

Dilophosaurus also had long, powerful legs and fairly short, strong arms. Each hand was four-fingered, although only three fingers had claws. **Dilophosaurus**'s tail was long and thick at the base, tapering toward the end.

These, then, are the features you would need to identify in order to be sure that a dinosaur you see in a book or exhibition is a **Dilophosaurus**:

For a meat-eater, **Dilophosaurus**'s jaws were fairly slender – some scientists have compared them with the jaws of a crocodile – and they were filled with thin, sharp teeth.

- two crests of bone on its head
- a flexible neck
- crocodilelike jaws
- short arms and four fingers, three with claws
- powerful legs
- a tapering tail

Crested skeleton

A female **Dilophosaurus**, whose crests were a duller color, would have been attracted by such bright crests.

Let's take a look at this illustration of a complete **Dilophosaurus** skeleton.

First, we'll examine those curious crests on top of its head. They were made of bone and were very thin.

In the male **Dilophosaurus**, scientists think it is possible that these head crests were very bright and colorful. They may have been used for display during mating season.

When alive, **Dilophosaurus** weighed nearly half a ton. Its skull was lightweight, and the jaws were weak. The jaws were probably used only to grab much smaller creatures.

When the scientist Samuel P. Welles gave a detailed description of **Dilophosaurus**, he also pointed out how large its skull was in proportion to its body, and that it had short arms and long legs.

The neck bones were thick and strong. They were probably attached to powerful muscles, giving **Dilophosaurus** the strength to turn its head easily, so that it could always be on the lookout.

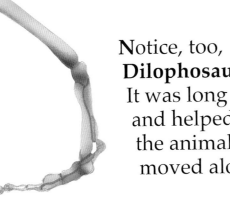

Notice, too, **Dilophosaurus**'s tail. It was long and strong and helped to balance the animal as it moved along.

When paleontologists are rebuilding skeletons from the remains that have been dug up, they can replace missing pieces with false bones made from fiberglass.

Sometimes a museum can make copies of a skeleton for other collections, perhaps in another country. They might sell them to an overseas museum or swap them for other skeletons that would be interesting for their collections.

And where can you see a **Dilophosaurus** skeleton? There is one on display at the University of California Museum of Paleontology in Berkeley, California. If that is too far away for you to visit, there may be a copy in a natural history museum nearer you.

Meat-eating scavenger

Dilophosaurus knew nothing about table manners! It was a fierce meat-eater, grabbing a large meal wherever it could find it.

But some scientists believe **Dilophosaurus** may have been more of a greedy scavenger than a hunter and predator.

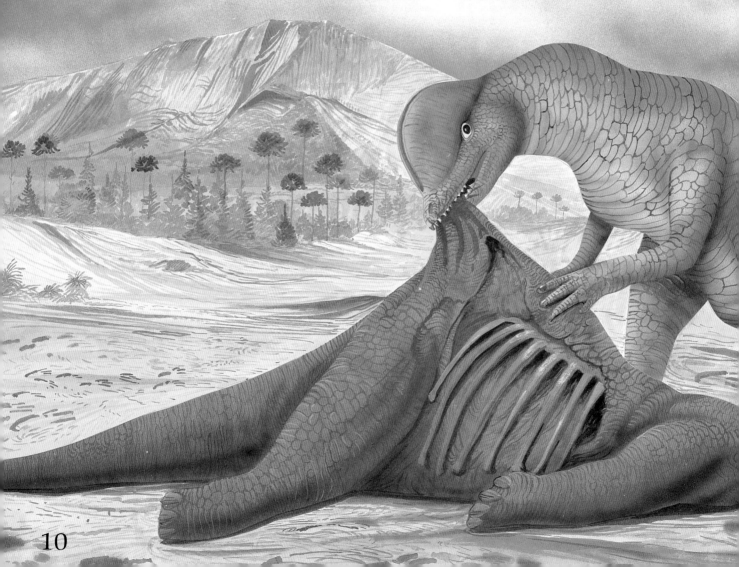

It may have preferred at times to eat dead animals it found lying around – such as the **Diplodocus** (DIP-<u>LOD</u>-OH-KUS) shown here – rather than killing its own supper. Scientists think this may have been the case because its jaws were not powerful enough to deal with any huge, violently struggling creatures.

Of course, if **Dilophosaurus** was very hungry and saw a small, tasty-looking creature – such as the armored, plant-eating **Scutellosaurus** (SKOOT-<u>EL</u>-OH-<u>SAW</u>-RUS), in the picture below – it would probably have gone after it right away! It might even have battled with another **Dilophosaurus** for it!

Dilophosaurus discovered

Finding the bones of dinosaurs is very exciting. And there was certainly great excitement when the remains of some dinosaurs were found in 1942 in northern Arizona.

They were discovered by a team of paleontologists from the University of California who had been shown the site by a Navajo Indian named Jesse Williams.

As the team members began to dig, they slowly uncovered the skeletons of three animals. One was almost complete, measuring about 20 feet (6 m) long. But it had no skull, so they could not tell what its head would have been like. The other two skeletons were in lots of pieces, and the bones had been worn away. Which type of dinosaur did the bones belong to?

The American paleontologist Samuel P. Welles worked very hard at putting the bones together but made quite a big mistake!

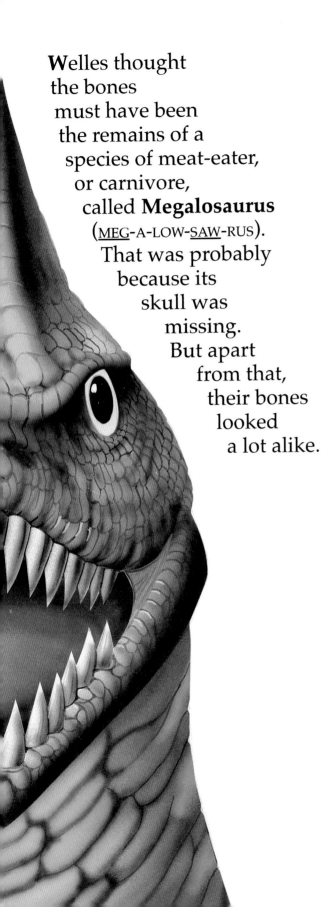

Welles thought the bones must have been the remains of a species of meat-eater, or carnivore, called **Megalosaurus** (MEG-A-LOW-SAW-RUS). That was probably because its skull was missing. But apart from that, their bones looked a lot alike.

Many years later, in 1964, Welles found another similar skeleton. This time, it was in better condition and had its skull, complete with a pair of bony crests. Welles now realized that it was a totally different creature from **Megalosaurus**.

Can you imagine all the excitement of finding it was an entirely new type of dinosaur? Welles and his team must have been thrilled. What a find!

Later, in 1970, Welles gave his dinosaur the name that we now know it by – **Dilophosaurus**, meaning "two-ridged lizard," because of the two crests on its head.

The hunt for more and new types of dinosaurs continues today all over the world. But large expeditions to remote parts of the globe are expensive to arrange.

What if *you* found a large skeleton of a fierce meat-eater? What would *you* name it?

13

Did dinosaurs swim?

Dinosaurs died out 65 million years ago, so there are a great many things about their lives that are now a mystery.

We can, however, learn much about them not only from their skeletons, but also from their footprints. But these can often raise big questions!

Dilophosaurus, for example, left lots of footprints in the ground that can be seen today. But some prints show marks left by just the tips of its claws. Surely this dinosaur could not have been walking on tiptoe?

What scientists believe is far more likely is that **Dilophosaurus** could swim a little.

Perhaps it had been crossing a stretch of water, and the claw-tips show where it had just touched the bottom of the lake or river.

Remember, though, that no dinosaurs ever lived all the time in water. They were land animals – but a few probably went into the water to hunt for fish, cool off, escape from predators, or simply cross a river.

Dinosaur teeth

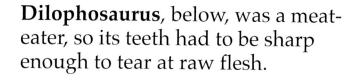

Dilophosaurus, below, was a meat-eater, so its teeth had to be sharp enough to tear at raw flesh.

But the teeth of carnivores (meat-eaters) were not all the same size. Usually, the biggest carnivores had the largest teeth.

The biggest dinosaur teeth found so far belonged to **Tyrannosaurus rex** (TIE-<u>RAN</u>-OH-SAW-RUS <u>RECKS</u>). Teeth that grew at the side of its mouth, near the front, were about the length of your lower leg, as you can see here, and were used for biting into prey.

By contrast with **Tyrannosaurus rex**, some small dinosaurs had teeth smaller than yours! **Troodon** (TROE-O-DON) – there are two of them in the third frame – had tiny, but incredibly sharp teeth; and if they had bitten you, this would have been very painful. In fact, the name **Troodon** means "wounding tooth."

In large carnivores, the curved edge of each tooth usually pointed backward. This gave them a better grip on their victims. Each tooth also usually had a serrated edge, like a saw, for cutting through meat. As the teeth wore away, they would be replaced by new ones growing up from below.

Plant-eating dinosaurs (herbivores) had teeth, too. But they were designed for coping with tough vegetation. Giants such as **Diplodocus** did not chew their food but used peglike teeth for raking leaves into their mouths, and then swallowing them right away.

Some duck-billed dinosaurs, such as **Edmontosaurus** (ED-MONT-OH-SAW-RUS), below, had an enormous number of teeth – a great many more than adult humans of today. Just imagine how long it would take to brush twice a day if *you* had that many!

Did Dilophosaurus spit?

In Steven Spielberg's wonderful film, *Jurassic Park*, there is a scary scene in which a **Dilophosaurus** suddenly aims a jet of dreadful-looking spit at Dennis Nedry. He is a computer expert in a dinosaur theme park who has stolen some dinosaur embryos from a laboratory. This spit contains a nasty poison.

But was **Dilophosaurus** – back in Early Jurassic times – *really* able to spit poison? Did it perhaps stun its prey this way? Scientists simply do not know.

Some animals living today, however, can certainly spit poison to defend themselves against enemies or to kill their prey. The most famous is the spitting cobra.

So maybe some dinosaurs *could* spit. The author of the book on which the film is based – Michael Crichton – suggested this and Steven Spielberg decided to include this possibility in his film. It certainly frightens most people who see the film, that's for sure!

The filmmakers also made their robotic **Dilophosaurus** look rather different from the reconstructions made by scientists who have dug up skeletons of this dinosaur.

The dinosaurs in the film are supposed to have been brought back to life by scientists working in a laboratory.

In bringing dinosaurs to the twentieth century, perhaps the scientists made some changes to them, too, giving **Dilophosaurus** a new appearance. Watch out! There could be one behind you. And it might just spit!

19

Dilophosaurus data

Scientists do not know for sure what the crests were for. They may have been brightly colored to attract females during the mating season. They may also have helped one **Dilophosaurus** recognize another. Perhaps, too, they had a part in controlling **Dilophosaurus**'s body temperature. But they were probably not used for fighting, since the bone was too delicate and may have shattered easily.

What a ferocious monster **Dilophosaurus** was! And how odd it looked! But it was probably lazy, often feeding as a scavenger. This meant it left other carnivores to kill prey and then enjoyed their leftovers.

Bony crests

The most striking feature about **Dilophosaurus** was at the top of its head. Here, there were two bony crests that looked like two halves of a dinner plate.

Large hands

Dilophosaurus's hands were large, and each one had four fingers. The first three were fairly long and had sharp claws for tearing meat from dead bodies. The fourth finger was short.

20

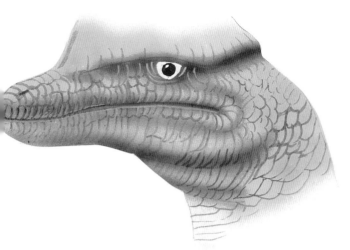

Slender jaws

For a meat-eating dinosaur, **Dilophosaurus** had unusually slender jaws that looked a little like those of a crocodile.

Because of this, some scientists think that it did not use its jaws for actually killing prey; instead, it may have relied on its hands for that grisly job. Then its jaws could take over and get down to the serious business of eating.

Thin, pointed teeth

Since **Dilophosaurus** was a meat-eater, it had very sharp teeth. Scientists have divided them into two groups. **Dilophosaurus** may have used the long, thin teeth at the front of its jaws for ripping meat off the remains of dinosaur carcasses (dead bodies) and then used those at the back for slicing up meat.

Slender tail

Dilophosaurus had a long, slender tail. When the animal ran, it held the tail stretched out behind it.

Meet some of the Theropods

Dilophosaurus (1) was a **Theropod** (THER-OH-POD), a two-legged, meat-eating dinosaur. There were several groups of **Theropods**.

Dilophosaurus belonged to a group called the **Ceratosaur** (SER-A-TOE-SAWR) gang. Now let's get to know some of the other **Theropods**.

The dinosaurs of the **Deinonychosaur** (DIE-NO-NIKE-OH-SAWR) gang were all light in build with vicious claws.

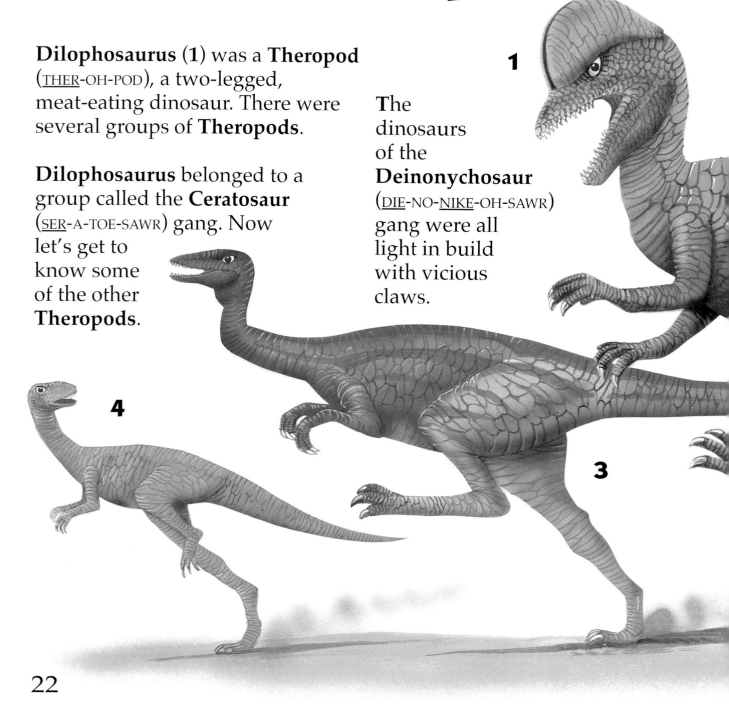

22

Velociraptor (VEL-<u>AH</u>-SI-<u>RAP</u>-TOR) (**2**) was perhaps the most ferocious member of the **Deinonychosaur** gang, from Late Cretaceous Mongolia. It is known for its great, sickle-shaped foot claws.

The most unusual **Theropods** belonged to the **Ornithomimosaur** (OR-<u>NITH</u>-OH-<u>MIME</u>-OH-SAWR) gang. **Ornithomimus** (OR-<u>NITH</u>-OH-<u>MIME</u>-US) (**3**) is from Late Cretaceous North America and Tibet.

Ornithomimus is sometimes called an "ostrich dinosaur" because it looks very much like an ostrich. It had a small head, toothless beak, and long, thin neck and legs. But it did not have feathers, and it had arms and a tail.

Among the smaller **Theropods** were members of the **Coelurosaur** (SEEL-<u>OO</u>-ROE-SAWR) gang, such as **Compsognathus** (<u>KOMP</u>-SOG-<u>NAY</u>-THUS) (**4**).

2

An earlier dinosaur from Late Jurassic Germany and France, **Compsognathus** was only about the size of a chicken and probably hunted in packs.

GLOSSARY

carnivores — meat-eating animals.

crest — a growth on top of an animal's head.

mate (v) — to join together (animals) to produce young.

pack — a group of similar or related animals that travels or hunts together.

paleontologists — scientists who study the remains of prehistoric creatures.

predators — animals that capture and kill other animals for food.

prey — an animal that is killed for food by another animal.

remains — a skeleton, bones, or a dead body.

scavenger — any animal that eats dead or decaying matter.

skeleton — the bony framework of a body.

INDEX